TRACES OF MY SOUL

APH MUSKI

this book is a very carefully curated collection of poems which tell a story. like any good story, there is drama, coming of age scenes, teenage angst [lots of angst], romance, self love, mythology, anything and everything that i could write a poem about to be honest. so prepare a drink of your choice, sit somewhere with warm lighting, play soft classical music, get comfortable and get started to encounter the traces of my soul, lovely reader. one more thing, take my poems with a grain of salt because everyone will perceive it differently, even me. well then, see you on the other side.

Contents

Contents

Contents

Acknowledgements

thank you to the people who made this book come to life. parents, teachers, muses, friends, artists and all others, i couldn't have done it without you.

—

chapter one: the cruel beginning

1. 11:11

the ceiling of clouds that rippled blood red in the night filled
with a glow, the reddish glow was mesmerizing and hellish all
at once;
hope was killed, and a flower was lost but *i felt free*.

ENDURE JUST A BIT MORE.

2. untitled

you know, sometimes i really hate myself. to be honest, it is
quite often that i find myself writhing in self-loathe.
when i am alone, fear sits beside me, carefully holds my hand
and says, "it is okay that everyone else is in twos and threes, i
will be here with you."
i reply, "it would be nice if i had friends too."
the world is just another name for despair.
it is an endless cycle of love and hate.
i am all of my joy, my pain and my anxiety.

hey you, the one looking in the mirror at four in the morning
whilst crying, how does it feel?
how does it feel when you know the world is closing in, but
you have to fight through it even though you have no will?
tell me, do you feel glad when you are piercing your soft
smooth skin?
do you feel the silver bite?
do you watch the sight of blood trickling down your arm in
agony or do you feel satisfied?
do you regret it all when you see the looks of the people you
love?
what do you do when you see their pity and disappointment
flashing in their eyes?

tell me, do you still remember the satisfaction you got when you felt the sweet yet tantalizing bite of the knife, when you knew that you've fallen in the eyes of your loved ones?
do you still feel that even though you might be loved, in the end you are alone?

3. one of those days

you know the days when you feel nothing but everything at
the same time?
when you're neither sad nor happy, when you don't know if
you should laugh or cry.
today is one of those days.

I miss the rain tapping against the window,
as if someone was knocking, asking for permission to come in.
even though I'm scared of the thunder,
there are days when I can actually like the sound,
because it makes me feel less lonely,
as if the loud booms of thunder resemble the loud beating of
my heart,
as if the howling of the wind tells me that I'm not the only
one in agony,
today is one of those days.

you know the days when you are finally ready to break down
all your walls,
you are ready to finally wear your heart on your sleeve,
you are ready to let your guard down and be defenseless but
there is no one there to listen?
today is one of those days.

4. drugged

dark room, lit up by blue lights,
her silhouette, sitting against the wall,
half passed out.

the empty syringe in her hand,
a droplet of blood trickling down her arm and now on the floor,
the only drug in her veins, melancholy.

your hunched figure stops outside her door,
you contemplate,
should you knock or just enter?
would she let you in?
"ah whatever", you think and go in.

she looks up at the intruder, you,
time comes to a standstill,
you gasp at her state,
her bloodshot eyes,
her puffy cheeks,
her haunting smile,
it was as if she was okay with everything that was going on.

she offers you a new filled syringe,
you refuse immediately,
she cocks her head to the side,
and raises her right brow,
you then realize that your life isn't all that better either.

you sigh and sit down beside her,
your shoulders touching,
the contact is not too much,
just enough,
"give me it", you say,
she happily complies.

you hiss when the irresistible drug enters your blood,
there in the dark room, lit up by blue lights,
a silent promise was made,
a promise that we will be sad and lonely,
together.

—

5. lypophrenic mind

should i have tried harder?
should i have changed myself?
would i love me then?
i really don't understand why humans are so obsessed with
roses,
why is it the flower of love when it is tainted red with the
blood of the dead lovers?
but i guess we see beauty in pain.
this full moon night,
i look at myself from the past,
i stand above my dead body,
it is covered in roses, the thorns piercing my skin.
all this time, i wonder,
why do they not like me?
why do i not like me?
is it because we only like to read about pain and not see it?
did they not see beauty in my pain?
was the blood seeping out of my already soft scarlet lips not
beautiful enough?
i was on my knees, crying tears of gold,
was that not beautiful?
should i have tried harder?
<u>would you love me then?</u>

6. cordolium

when i see you my heart does a somersault
but when i see you look at her, the same heart cries.
you chose her and i don't blame you,
she is like aphrodite reincarnated,
her amaranthine locks,
her orphic irises,
her elysian beauty.
i love her as well but in a different way than you,
i will never get infuriated at her because you chose her,
instead,
i hate that i am in love with you,
i might love you but i don't like you.
this is what the french call,
"la douleur exquise".

7. love unreturned

love unreturned
i wish you would look at me the way you look at her.
why?
because it is getting difficult to just play along with your antics
when all i want to do is cry.
that's why.
i have never felt this way before, did you know that?
never have felt like a hypocrite, not taking my own advice.
do you know how many nights i have spent trying to make
sense of these feelings?
do you know about those late night phone calls, when they
tried to warn me to not fall, not this time?
but i did and it hurt.

i wish you would look at me the way you look at her.
she just has to exist and your cheeks get flushed,
your pupils dilate,
one flair of her hand makes your heart flip,
and there's me, standing in the corner of the room, head held
low,
the crown on my head falls down at my feet.

sometimes, late at night,

i wish you weren't my friend,

it would have been less tiring to move on from you,

don't you worry,

i will get soon over this love unreturned, but,

oh, how i wish you would look at me the way you look at her.

8. the devil's hour

it is 3 a. m.
the so called devil's hour,
but isn't the only devil here, me?

oh no, don't avert your eyes,
look at me,
i said look at me!

come, join me, as i sit down in front of the mirror,
blade in hand,
ready to die.

"please don't do it", you beg,
you know i am not going to listen to you, so why even try?
"please don't."

i raise the blade,
the light reflects,
i put it near my neck,
eyes gleaming with unshed tears,
i cut, with all my might.

you let out a blood curdling scream,

you sob on my body,
my hands caress your cheek, tainting it with my blood,
"you'll be okay", i say.

at 3 a. m.,
the so called devil's hour,
the devil in me died along with your innocence.

—

chapter two: the subtle realization

9. i shouldn't

she thought she was finally over it,

was finally over her hating herself,

was finally over succumbing to the thoughts in her head,

the voices that finally stopped,

there was no more ringing in her ears,

there were no more nights of deafening silences, when
sometimes you could hear sobs coming from a girl who grew
up too soon.

but they all returned,

the returned with a vengeance.

the girl who was supposed to hear the birds chirping in the
clear sky,

could only hear the loud voices in her head telling that she is
not beautiful,

that she'll never be good enough.

for a while, she listens,

she listens to these voices that tell her the "truth" about
herself,

and she believes them.

suddenly,

her own voice rises above,

"i shouldn't, i shouldn't listen to them."

after that day,

her smile grew again,

her heart had finally won over her mind,

she was ready to love herself,

the voices are still there,

but they are muted in front of her beautiful voice.

10. scarlet carnations

her light is not wrathful like the noonday sun,
it doesn't make your skin feel like a flaming tiger lily,
instead, it envelopes you like a silk robe you'd wear in the early
morning,
but if you get too close, you might even get burnt,
i have scars from loving her, and there is nothing i would do
to change that.

her voice, it can either be dead as a wilted sunflower or fruity
as a watermelon in warm summer nights.
she makes you pay her attention for she likes it,
you are instantly mesmerized, curious to what she'll say next.
the disdain in her voice is almost comical, the way she slurs
her words when someone has let her down yet again,
would make you want to hunt the person who dare hurt this
sweetheart.

her face is just oh so beautiful,
the way her eyes smile when someone reacted exactly the way
she wanted when she cracked a poor joke,
the pure joy she radiates when she's with the people she truly
loves,
the way her nose crinkles in disgust,

the way a soft blush taints her cheeks when the person she
likes looks at her,
her eyebrows, which already have a natural slit and,
the ones she cried because they weren't good enough,
they raise up in amusement or a challenge,
with her, you either become her soulmate or get intimidated
and run away without looking back.

her mind, honestly it would scare you sometimes,
the way it switches from sunshine and kittens to bloody
carnage.
she knows everything,
i mean every single thing,
she knows the way you lie,
she knows the way you love her,
she knows the way she loves herself,
she knows.

what she doesn't know is that how it hurts you when she says
that she is easy to hate,
she is not.
it is just so easy to love her,
why wouldn't a sane person love an insane one?
the more you spent time with her,
she'll make you insane, about her.
you'll be surprised at how well you get along for that you both
are absolutely different,

as time passes, all the differences will fade away and only the similarities will remain.

her sanguine aura and your, cerulean

come together and became a enchanting iris hue.

—

11. mi amor

you're the one i come to when im at the lowest point in life,

but you become my wings so i can fly.

you're my everything.

honestly, this statement scares me,

how can one person be everything?

but you are.

your eyes which are a deep black,

it reminds me of the universe if didn't have any stars,

the stars start freckling the dark when you talk about the things you love,

your jokes, your art, your precious doggos,

i looked in your eyes and learned the meaning of stargazing.

i will say i love you to you over and over again until it's just a senseless babble,

i will say i love you to you over and over again until it's just a senseless babble.

12. safe space

you and me,
dancing slowly to the croons of lana del rey,
in the middle of the night,
the room lit up by moonlight.
your hands on my waist,
gently holding me close,
my head on your chest,
your heartbeats are quick,
i smile and ask, "am i making your heart race?"
you grimace at the cheeky question but still nod,
"it is you, always will be you"
i stand on my toes and kiss you softly,
you smile against my lips.
i slowly whisper the words that you'd never thought i would
say, "i love you"
your eyes widen,
chuckling i say it again, "i love you, my love"
your hands pulls me in again for a kiss,
but this time it's more passionate,
we can feel the love in the way we kiss.
oh how i wish we could stay like this forever.

13. moonsong

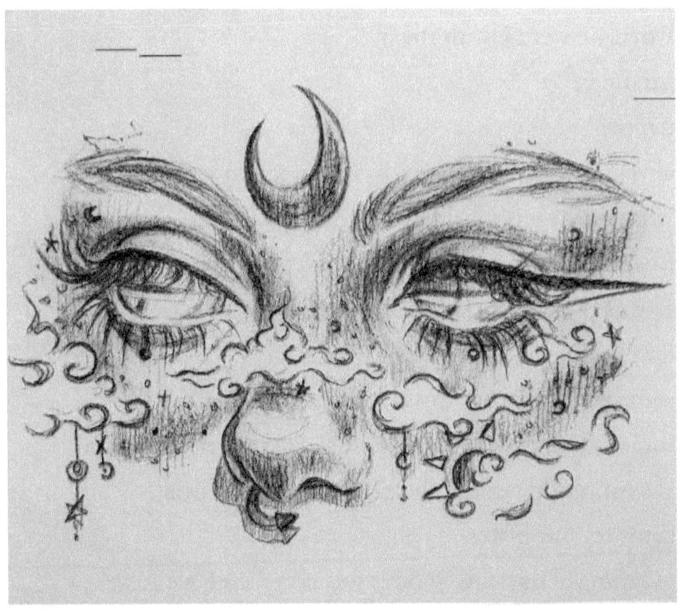

tonight, i lay down under the dark eerie sky
the only light is coming from her, the moon
she stands over me, protecting my heart from the cruel world
i long to touch her,
to be held in her arms like a long lost lover.

14. canteen's rajma chawal

i miss those days,
when we were just thirteen,
carefree,
happy,
always complaining about wanting to grow up,
what do we wish for now?
to go back,
to those fridays,
that particular part of the school stage,
some people sitting cross legged,
some standing, leaning against the person next to them,
almost messily eating the canteen rajma chawal,
three to four plates,
moaning about how good it was every time we ate it,
laughing too loud,
running after each other,
then
the canteen wala uncle left,
and a new one came,
rajma chawal was removed from the menu,
years passed,
it was added again,
but it wasn't the same,

as we ate it with a frown on our faces in the last year of school,

desperately trying to recreate those happy times,

one question in all our minds,

"did we grow up too soon?"

—

chapter three: the young lovers

15. yearning in the late night

aren't all lovers a bit broken hearted? waiting by the window, in the moonlit night for that one faint brush of hands, that one embrace which takes your breath away, that one soft kiss, saying the words in silence "i found you"

16. blame cupid

i ached for him, badly,

i need him.

his hands caressing my body, cherishing it,

his lips on mine,

my hands pulling at his soft hair,

i like to think that he feels the same way,

that he feels this chemistry between us,

that sometimes at night, he thinks about me like i think about
him,
but i know he is not.
i pick up the phone and dial that oh so familiar number,
"hey cupcake, miss me already?"
his voice sounds so emotionless sometimes,
"shut up", i say and shake my head furiously even though he
can't see me.
"same place?" he asks,
"and at the same time."
when twilight comes, he knocks at my door.
i open it and look at him as if i am a lovesick fool,
"i am sure this was against protocol but i love the way my
hoodie looks on you, kitten"
i just hug him, tightly,
his chest rumbles with laughter, "you really cannot wait, can
you?"
i shake my head no,
he picks me up and takes me to the couch.
there i was, in his arms, safe,
being with him felt like home,
he was running his hands through my badly dyed hair,
i don't remember telling him that i liked him doing that,
but he knows,
somehow, he knows everything.
we talk and talk,
we're comfortable in each other's skin,

after a while, the grandfather clock chimed,
it had already been an hour,
i knew what he was going to say before he opened his mouth,
"i know you have to go but can't you just stay tonight?"
"angel..."
"please, just stay,"
"let me go, kitten." i don't like when he is authoritative so i let
go, almost immediately,
i drop my head and refuse to look at him,
"look at me, petal"
i look at him with teary eyes,
i tried so hard to blink them away but they just won't go,
he kisses me on the forehead and ruffles my hair,
"i will see you next time"
"please"
"you know i can't. i have other clients waiting for me and
they are crazy about me. well, i am that good, you know?" he
smirks,
"you are just a conceited bastard."
"a bastard that you love, my little cupcake."
with that he closes the door behind him and walks away.
why can't it just be real?
why did i fall for the one person, i am not supposed to fall for?
he is just good at doing his job, he doesn't love me.
blame cupid for this wrongdoing.

17. snippets of love

i have a wounded heart,
it is incomplete,
only your kiss can complete me.

i tell you that i love you because i don't have anything else to
say,
i don't know how to explain the storm in my heart which rages
on and on
the waves crash on the land of my soul
seeking for solace,
the only solace ever found will be in your arms.

18. shot by his arrow

"ouch!" she yelped as she felt a blinding pain in her chest. she looked down to see an arrow piercing her heart?! "what the heck?? did someone really shoot me with an arrow?" "i'm so so sorry, love", a voice like honey muttered slowly. she saw a boy with angelic skin and a bow in his hands. he was looking down at his feet, clearly ashamed. " did you shoot me?" the boy started to nod his head, before he could say anything she interrupted him, "how? why? what? why do you look like cupid? is this some twisted prank?" "please calm down, love and let me explain" he touched her arm and miraculously her breathing turned back to normal, her heart slowed down and her adrenaline wasn't sky high anymore. "i look like cupid because i am. no, i am not lying and please don't freak out." "i didn't even say anything" "i can read your mind" he said matter-of-factly. his hand was still on hers, that's why she didn't yell and shriek and scream. "okay...i believe you, not sure why but i do. i have questions" her own voice shocked her, it was breathy and soft, much unlike how she usually spoke. "i'm sure you do and i'll do my best to answer them. please know that im extremely apologetic, i wasn't paying attention for you got shot." his manner of talking was in stark contrast to how he looked, you would expect a cheery bubbly voice that spoke immature thoughts out loud, instead, it was a honey dew tone which spoke like he had lived for a long time and experienced every single thing.

"first of all, we can't sit here like this, people will see us." "oh do you want me to change?" "change how?" a strong breeze suddenly blew in her face which made her eyes close for a fleeting moment and when she opened them she saw a guy who was just beautiful.
he smiled and said "you should close your mouth, sweetheart" she hadn't realized that she was gaping at this Roman God, quite literally, and quickly composed herself. "would this be okay? i don't want to cause any more trouble than i already have." "yes it's more than okay! i mean it's fine i guess." he laughed a hearty laugh, "you're not in love with me, sweetheart don't forget that"

"anyway...how is this arrow still in my chest but i'm not bleeding at all?" she quickly asked to change the subject. he replied, "the arrow of love doesn't make your already bleeding heart bleed more, i am not that cruel." "okay? and it hurts a bit, it is not killing me slowly, right?" "love brings you pain, sure, but it won't kill you. the intensity of the pain you're feeling is at a very low level because you're not with someone you love. it will be at its highest when you're in direct contact with 'The One." "okay so tell me, who is it? so i know who to avoid" "oh that's not how it works i'm afraid." "so i have to walk around with this stupid arrow piercing my heart?"

"precisely." "cupid!!!" "no one can see it except the one who loves you. don't you worry, doll, i will be here to help you at all times, Scout's honor." she smiled, "wow didn't know the stupid God of love had a sense of humor" "hey! that's not very nice of you!" "was shooting an arrow through my heart nice?" "touché."

jump to a few days later when she had just gotten used to the subtle pain in her chest, but something had to have happened because why should things sail smoothly? she met him, the moment he hugged her like he always did, the pain in her chest had reached an unbearable height. she was doubled over in pain and he was getting frantic to see why this cute little girl was in so much pain. she had to quickly think of an excuse so the best one she could come up with was period cramps, "cramps" she croaked out. she pretended that she was fine and now she was actually getting used to it again, she didn't have the heart to go home when she knew he was so excited to be with his friend. ouch that hurt, is she his friend? turns out he was excited for sure, but he wanted to share some news. "sooo you know i was talking to this girl and i kinda liked her? we are dating now." her heart sank and she didn't even know why. she said her congratulations and excused herself saying that her cramps were getting worse.

she practically ran to her house, wanting to cry freely in front of her walls, who accept her every emotion no matter how unreasonable they seem. she opened her door and there he was, grown up cupid, he had a solemn expression on his sculpted face. she realized he knew, of course he knows he's a freaking god. "love, stop thinking and let your feelings take over for once please." she ran to him and he welcomed her with open arms. she cried and cried, in his arms, she cried so much that she felt like she would drown any second. "i'm so sorry, it's my fault" she didn't say anything and he accepted. she thought about a lot of things and didn't even need to say them out loud for he could read minds, stupid god. she tried and she finally saw the silver lining, at least she could be close to him and he would be happy, that's all that matters. "how are you being optimistic whilst you're crying? you're a strange human, sweetheart" "that's just the way i am, stupid cupid" she replied with a smile and his heart felt at ease. she came to terms with the pain because she understood that there is a type of love only experienced through pain. she was always there for him whenever he needed her, she would let him playfully mock her shyness, not knowing she's shy because she's in love with him, she would let him take her out to see weird films which she didn't really understand, she let him rant about his family, his problems because that's the least she could do, she was even there for him in his sadness when he parted ways with his partner. he didn't know that she would just stare at him admiring him, not in a creepy way though, she would laugh at his poor (read endearing) attempts at acting cute. he was not Jupiter nor Apollo, he didn't need to be some God for her to love him, he didn't know that she would do anything for him.

cupid had even offered to shoot him with his arrow but she refused saying that it wouldn't be fair. "what do you want me to do? i will do anything! i really want you to feel better, sweetheart." "oh stop lamenting, dear cupid. i will be fine i promise." one night when bacchus or gaea had decided that they would torment her with the loud booms of lightning, the rattling of the windows and howling of the wind, he showed up at her door. he let himself in and called out for her, "cupcake, i came because i know you are scared of the thunder. where are you?" "coming!!" she yelled from her room where she was talking with cupid. cupid knowingly smiled; he knew what was going to happen and he wanted to witness that. she came out rushing, in her sweatshirt. he looked shocked at her appearance apparently "what happened? do i look bad?" "no no you look perfect as always but muffin?" "yes?" "why are you walking around with an arrow puncturing your pretty heart?" "you can see the arrow?!" her voice was raising with each syllable. "yes i can. is this a weird cosplay or something? because you're not bleeding" "shut up" "excuse me?" "i said stop talking," he fake gasped, "oh shush and would you please try to remove the arrow?" "are you sure you're not hurt, cupcake? i hate seeing you get hurt" "hey hey, i'm not hurt and you won't hurt me so take out the arrow please" he did it while grimacing of course and when it was completely out she fell into his arms. he didn't know what to do so he kissed her forehead like he always did. she knew he was listening intently, so she let him know "i don't blame you anymore, stupid cupid."

19. how did you know it was love

how did you know it was love?
it was quite simple for me to realise that what i felt for him, was indeed love.

it was when the image in my head after reading my own poem was just his face,

the lines of my poetry being the lines on his face; the laugh lines, the way his brows furrow in worry,

the sweet words that flow easily out my heart being the honey that drips from his lips,

the warmth that i feel while reading poetry being the warmest of hugs i have ever experienced by just looking into his eyes,

the yearning, the pang in my heart which i used to feel like reading poetry is not there anymore because i gave away my heart to him.

20. moonrise at 4:23 AM

<u>he is everything</u>
but everyone says, "don't be so cliche"
she screams at them to keep quiet
he is that november sun; not harsh but oh so warm, pulling
me into an embrace, she says
he is my favorite poem; which i tear up reading even though i
have read it countless of times before,
he is that gentle april breeze which makes the sunflowers sway
in the eve
but,
he is also the lightning i am so afraid of, i fear he'll strike me
down any second.
"oh you foolish child! run away from him and never look
back!"
but it would be an honor to die from his hands, she spoke
with strange yearning
oh! what a sight it would be! his heart enveloping mine.
i don't want nothing else, just his heart.
and she got it,
no matter what they said, she stayed,
in his arms, till she breathed her last breath,
<u>*giving away her heart to her lover to keep.*</u>

21. old tapes on repeat

do you remember when we first met?
you were waiting for me,
it felt like an eternity
was it that i stood you up?
but i could never

we finally met
i was sitting and you walked in
my heart quickened, palms sweaty,
throat parched, starstruck
should i get up? or just act cool?
should i hug you? would it be too much?
questions questions questions

you came in like a fresh gust of wind and left like a storm
you gave me candies, a photo as a parting gift,
in return i gave you a poem and myself
after you left, i was stared at,
it was almost as if they judged me for giving away my heart
and soul to you so easily
or
did they know something that i didn't?
did they know i was already in too deep?

did my love for you begin that day?

i don't mind if these questions are left unanswered,
the only question that matters is, "do you love me?"
and i know the answer, you do.

22. destined

[destined]
i didn't fall for you,
nor you did for me,
i flew down to the ground,
trying to find a purpose,
just as i reached,
my feet were sinking in the quicksand,
i wasn't trying to come up,
i saw you look up to me from down below,
you were sitting cross legged in the darkest of dark places,
i sat down in front of you,
imitating your every move,
you smiled loudly,
it wasn't a laugh yet,
it was the first time i heard a sound like that,
i wanted to hear it over and over again,
i was unabashedly staring at you,
you were staring back,
you said,
"if you're trying to find my soul or my heart, you're not going
to find them"
i reply,
"i know already because they're with me"

i urge you to find my heart and soul,
you cannot,
after a moment, you gasp,
"they're with me"
yes they are,
your heart in my chest, mine in yours,
we're made of each other,
for each other,
for love.

23. even hell feels heavenly with you, my love

the night was as dark as he claimed his soul was,

the air smelt like candles in the church,

the bells were tolling,

she was there, waiting in her sadness,

he walked over,

why would you do it? she asked

because i couldn't live without you anymore,

as they met, again,

chaos resumed, a storm began,

they had touched death and smiled at him,

in turn, he blessed them,

as they walked away, hand in hand,

the night grew darker as the candles blew out.

—

chapter four: the cracks in the dinner plates
and trying to mend them

24. coward in love

you said that i was an angel
you were the demon
i belonged in heaven,
you in hell,
a love never seen before,
i promised you
i'll fight my way to hell, if that means to stay with you
i am here, lost in the darkness
i can't seem to find you anywhere
"poor child" i hear the devil say
i look up to him, unafraid
after all why would i be afraid in my home,
hell is a home for the heartless and you ran away with mine.

25. questions for the devil

"what a cruel cruel world!"
you yell this at the top of your voice every single night,
let me ask you, "does it do you any good?"

"no it doesn't", you mumble back,
"but i despise the way this world works,
humans are always out for blood, they hurt, they kill,
themselves or others",
you say,
"let me ask you, are you pleased with this world?"

"no of course not, why would i be?
but it doesn't mean that i am not in love with it",
my voice is raising above yours, not loud but it's making you
listen,
"these humans you speak of as malicious menaces are actually
just forbidden somber souls, trying to survive,
let me ask you, have you ever thought about it this way?"

"your silence is deafening", i remark,
"say your thoughts out loud, no matter how
scalding they might be",

"what about the ones who hurt children? the ones who hurt
animals?"
my breath hitches, the corners of your mouth raise, you say,
"let me ask you, is it really worth it to be scorched by the
hedonic corrupt agony?"

"it is worth it", i reply vehemently,
"it is worth it when i see these humans stop at the roadside to
capture the moment when they saw a flower bloom,
when their pretty irises light up like the universe when they
see animals,
when their hearts have been broken and they let out wails of
anguish and they try to heal by drinking the smoldering elixir,
when a child borns, all the distress the mother felt fades away
instantly when she hears the cries of her beautiful child,
when poets puts everyone's emotions into words,
when a lover uses the same lines for his significant other,
let me ask you, what do you have to say now?"

"i don't have anything to say anymore", you whisper in defeat,
"but,
let me ask you, these humans associate you with the blood
curdling, appalling desolate evil so why are your thoughts
achingly hopeful?"
i smile but my eyes water with the torment,
"because i yearn for the light too sometimes."

26. the aftermath

eh? what is happening? wasn't i just watching a random youtube video moments ago? so why are there tears all over my cheeks now? why isn't my hand moving to wipe them off? why is my chest hurting? no it's my heart, why is it hurting so much? why am i clinging onto the pillow as if it's someone i know? why am i trying to get it to hug me back? why aren't my tears stopping? it's been ten minutes already, right? why won't you stop then? why isn't anyone coming to help me? why isn't god here? isn't god supposed to be all knowing? is he just ignoring me now? why am i asking such questions? why can't i move? why can't i stop? did i do something wrong? why is my heart hurting? why does it feel like my lungs are being crushed? do i deserve this? why can't i do anything about it? did i do something wrong? did i do something wrong? why does it hurt? did i do something wrong? did i do something wrong? i can't breathe

27. dear autumn

do you know me?
do you remember me?
do you remember those times?
the nights i cried,
the nights i smiled,
the nights you cried,
the nights you smiled,
why? why me? why you? why us?
why are we trying to kill each other?
why are you trying to break me?
i was called heartless when you knew that it was with you,
i asked you to keep it as your own,
you promised,
now you stepped on that promise like it was a dry leaf which
shattered under you,
my heart in your clenched fist, bleeding
you drop it to the ground,
i was barely able to stand,
ready to collapse, you
held me close,
intertwined our hands,
my blood on fingertips,
then you left,

autumn, you have been cruelly cold to me this time,

with the same blood i write you this letter,

you won,

you've always won

but at what cost?

you used to be the one i thought of when i read the word

"love"

now i can't forgive you for what you did,

for leaving me in the cold,

the fallen leaves marking my knees as a reminder of how it is

to love you,

i despise you

28. the frailty of time

in january i told you that i loved you

in february in the early hours of the day you softly said that you loved me too

in july, I'll fall to my feet swearing that i never wanted to grab the knife and put it to your veins

i just wanted to save our lives somehow

in august, i constantly told you as if to remind you that i do indeed love you

in september, the phrase began to feel like a poor attempt to not let the other leave

in october you stopped saying it

in november you stopped feeling it

the last march we couldn't stop confessing our love

this march, you said that you only felt disgust

you also said you never felt that our love was bad for you

why would you always leave me confused?

the remaining days of march, i realised i never stopped feeling it, i hadn't said it out loud in so long that it felt that the love was gone

this april, I'll tell you

i never regretted meeting you, loving you, making you my muse

i only regret us getting caught up in the webs of hurt

i will walk away from you even though it breaks me
but being with you in the end also did the same
throughout the months of may till september
i will try not to think about you, about what we were and
what we became
in september, you'll wish me a happy birthday
maybe you'll even add "i hope you're taking care"
the conversation will end in a few texts
in november, I'll do the same to you
the conversation will end in one text
in december, in the last moments of the year
I'll catch myself promising that we would still be in love in
another life

doriana

29. a vulnerable conversation between ares and aphrodite;heartbreak and healing

U did cut me
Saw me bleed
But looked away
Now u come with a bandage,
Trying to help
The wound almost healed
But now scratched off, so
Here I bleed again
Hoping u won't look away.

i saw you bleeding,
looked away not knowing it was me holding the knife,
i'm coming in to help
now you're bleeding,
did i do it again?
but i won't look away,
I'll be here to stay,
gently kissing the hundred paper cuts

and we'll bring us back to life

i used you without even knowing,
i held on to the knife as if i was stuck,
i threw it away now,
we both are covered in blood,
but we'll wash it off,
adorn the wounds with flowers,
the wounds heal,
our hearts heal and once again, filled with love

Wounds do heal u say
I believe
What I don't believe is they aren't stubborn enough to kill us
with their marks
The knife u held
The cuts u made
The blood that spilled
The doors u closed
The doors u didn't
The nights that cried
The moons that shined
I would go through everything again if I knew it would b
better
So I stopped.

i believe it would get better

so i don't want us to stop
the knife replaced with a pen,
the cuts with words,
the wounds with kisses,
the closed doors always open,
the sun shining the light on your teary face,
the moon giving her blessings,
death embracing us but letting go for it isn't our time yet

"i'll love you when i love you. i'll love you when i like you. i'll love you when i don't like you. i'lll love you when i hate you. i'll be here when you love me. i'll be here when you like me. i'll be here when you don't like me. i'll be here when you hate me. because i'll be living in our love and you will too. they tell me not to start a sentence with because but i will for it's not the beginning nor the end."

30. a page out of my diary

no one ever tells you what happens after love

love never leaves

love always finds a way to have its foot in the threshold of your home

it's the shadow that almost never leaves

i can sense it throughout the day

but it vanishes when night comes

that's when i truly feel alone

love is the person you have stopped talking to but didn't think you would

when talking every single day turns into thinking that getting a text after weeks is a treasure

the person leaves and tries to take away the love

but no one can

it'll stay as the knowledge i have about what makes them, them

the way they can't sit still

how they look over at your sleeping figure with utmost fondness

when they claim that they aren't good with words but still make you swoon with one sentence

the times where i eat something with ketchup, i get reminded how they hate it and will act like a nauseous cat

and how i can't afford to smile at that anymore
the way i now have a distaste for the month of June
and living through November is too painful
love never leaves
the fond looks turn into betrayed faces
the sweet words turn into daggers
everywhere we touch, we hurt
but we don't stop trying to heal each other
sweet words are said again
love is shared again
alas! the memories of the dagger twisting in your soul never
stops replaying
in the end
both of us are bloody
barely breathing
how did we get here?
in our last breath as what the world would know as lovers
we confess
love did almost turn into hate
we never let it
we never would ever regret it
but it never left
now we both are alive again but not
both sensing the same things because we always thought that
we were connected
i would like to think that their life flashes by their eyes
whenever someone mentions poetry and muses

like mine does when i see art or someone says anything about

greek gods

years have gone by

but love stays as the ever burning candle in the darkened room

31. a summer story

夏の話 a summer story

the sun of our story already set last summer,

but the fragments of your sunshine still pierce me,

tell me how am i supposed to not like an orchid that

desperately needs that sliver of light to bloom.

the promise of always and forever long forgotten,

i found our always clinging on to my legs begging me to not leave and

saw forever get crushed in your pretty hands.

goodbye is what i wish i could have said but,

i thought that the summer sun was too harsh on us, was it not?

now i wander aimlessly in the rain,

with my heart in my hands beating as loud as the thunder,

look what we did, thunder doesn't even scare me anymore,

all i am doing is looking for someone to take my heart again and mend it,

but i never will find that one for all i always want is you.

that's all there is to this story,

you took away my soul in the summer,

let it melt and gave back the remains,

even if our love lost its meaning along the way,

i will keep it with me <u>always</u>
and the traces of my soul will <u>forever</u> stain your hands.

32. almost

why don't you do it? you already have your dagger pressed
against my throat, just a bit more and i would bleed
why are you coming closer? please just go away if you aren't
planning on my death
our foreheads touch ever so slightly,
shaky breaths, the blade still there,
i close my eyes unable to look into your piercing eyes
anymore,
i can feel you thinking, i can feel it in the way the blade
shivers,
a small droplet on my cheek
you're crying, i thought we aren't supposed to show emotions
i finally gather the courage to look at you
i don't know what it was that made you recoil
could you see love?
"no don't look at me like you love me"
"but i do"
"you aren't supposed to"
"you are supposed to kill me, do that then"
"don't play with my head"
you come closer again, the dagger back at my throat,
the blade doesn't shiver anymore

"you love me and you're too afraid to accept that you're capable of love"
the blade pushes in, rupturing my skin
"i have no choice im sorry"
you won't win,
you never will,
you'll still be the villian every single time,
and i would be the hero who died in love.

33. a letter from aphrodite to ares and back//in another life

my hands are shaking as i write my thoughts

im too tipsy,

shouldn't drink that much,

but i couldn't stop myself from pouring it all

am i drowning my sorrows?

i'll let you decide

there's music playing, i don't know the song,
don't know what it is that reminds me of you
in another life,
i'll be your girl,
we'll keep all our promises,
be us against the world
in another life,
i will make us stay
so we don't have to say we were the ones that got away,
the ones that got away
i didn't even try to think of you,
but you came in my mind like the lord you are,
sometimes it feels like im being watched by you,
i rememberthe time we both met,
when i was nervous and you loved the way i was,
hesitantly i hugged you but you didn't let me go
in another life,
i'll be your boy,
i'll get better and will stand beside you,
in another life,
we will make us stay
so we don't have to say we were the ones that got away,
the ones that got away
i open my eyes and i see you crying with me,
in my dreams, i see you kissing me,
in poetry, i see you smiling at me,
now i'll drown myself in your love,

cause in another life,

i will be your love,

you'll kiss my mind and I'll kiss you on your heart,

in another life,

we will stay together always and forever,

we won't let go,

we won't let go.

chapter five: the anger seeping out of the cracks

34. pain undeserving

seven hours of pain you said,

the pain you wanted,

because it meant that you'll have me,

but mother, why won't you want me anymore?

the child you wanted to be an angel, even so a god,

is this all i am for you?

aren't you tired of punching my gut? my heart? my mouth?

isn't the dried blood enough to make you stop?

"i am doing it out of love" you say while crying,

if this is the way i get your love,

i will taste your tears and my blood out of your hand,

every seven days, you pluck out feathers from my wings,

it hurts every single time,

is it to remind us of the pain you felt when you had me?

how will i ever be an angel when i don't even know anything

else but to fall?

why? why did you turn me into the devil when you wanted a

god?

35. to the person i'd like to say fuck you to

i cannot take your name because whenever i do, i get reminded that we share the same blood,

your blood pumps through my heart. as if it wasn't enough for you to stain my skin, your blood taints my heart,

that realization makes me tear my skin with my bitten nails; slowly pick through the veins and arteries; snip them off one by one; and watch as my innocence, my childhood, your love drains out,

i would do all this, go through immense pain just so i could declare that we don't share the same blood anymore,

you would find me peacefully lifeless on the floor; a flushed smile on my face; wearing white surrounded by rotting tones of vermilion and scarlet that feel like fire beneath your feet,

you would be hesitant in touching me,

your trembling hands reach for my cheek and you almost mistake me for being alive,

dead bodies that are left alone for long are supposed to be cold you might think,

you will never be able to forget this slight touch because it will finally sink in that,

even though you thought you took everything from me, **you could never take away my warmth.**

36. the tale of the chosen one and the outcast

your body is a vessel where i keep all my inhibitions hidden
under the skin
i know you're swallowing your words back in by that look in
your eyes,
speak child, i am not that cruel that i will do away with your
tongue like they tried to do with mine

why us?

don't you get it, sweet one?
we are the *fallen*
we rose from the ashes of my own bones

they all talk about the devil and how he is the worst kind of
entity in this universe,
no don't look at me like that, they do!
you haven't seen the light in so long so you don't know what
they say nowadays

but oh my dear
little do they know

they've dined with her, eaten the food that she made, laughed
with her, gave her their hearts,

you were cast away, they made you the devil!
you stayed here and i
i crawled back up and they made me the chosen one
the god of their lands
whatever that means
we will show them, little one
that our cruelty is the mercy they deserve

if all hell breaks loose and these demons who only resemble
humans
come waging war
i will fight

i will fight too

that is how i want to die,
with you by my side
let the world fall into the depths of despair just like they threw
us down
hold hands while the flames engulf us whole
into the realm of freedom solely made for us because at last
the devil stopped caring and the god lost all her inhibitions.

37. a voicemail from the banished son, the fallen angel

hey it's me again,
you know what?
i have gotten used to the endless ringing
when i call you,
the point where i'm supposed to
start leaving my message after the beep,
the beep somehow feels nostalgic,
then i remember where i heard it,
in the hospital with you but,
the beeping sound was in a single note and longer,
how could i not get familiar with it?
i can't stop picking up the phone in my shaking heavy hands
and dialing your number,
and you can't stop not picking up.

come back to this place
we're supposed to call home,
it's not the way it used to be,
but you understand, right?
that *i had to* do what i did,

people talk as if i hated you,
why would i offer your favorite flowers
at your grave then?
i have started to miss you,
i don't think i should,
at least that's what others tell me,
come back,
let me be the one who falls to my death,

i wonder if these were the sights
you saw after you ruined me everyday,
what was going on in your mind when
you were *stripping me of my innocence?*
every time i look down at my hands,
they're covered in your blood,
did you see me in the mirror
all bruised up like i do you?
do i cry with *guilt like you* or
do i smile a *smile tainted with betrayal?*

the food doesn't taste the same
without your love and disappointment,
come back and love me again,
at least *try to* this time around,
if making a house out of my skin and bones
is what makes it a home,
kill me then,

just please,

love me.

until next time, my guardian,

who failed to be a protector and became my punisher instead.

38. i'll let the fire burn me brighter

my love died,

i lost it, somewhere along the way.

love is not supposed to be a competition,

but why did i lose?

how can i keep on losing every game i play?

my legs can't keep bearing the weight

of my

loneliness anymore,

the edge of the cliff is right within my reach,

do i fall here, on the safe ground or endure a bit more and fall

down the pits of despair, the only home i've ever known?

i think i'll go back home tonight,

the fall is soft, gentle on my body

long arms emerge from the earth to hold me close,

they stroke my hair and

let me rest my head against their chest,

i can't hear a heartbeat,

i never could

but somehow this entity was more humane

than *everyone else.*

tonight, their grip on me is tighter,
with a hint of plea and desperation
you don't want me to go?
their hand stops playing with my hair and i knew,
i won't go.
a home filled with solitude is better than people who masquerade
as my lovers.

the hand starts moving again,
lulling me to sleep
even in my dreams, the question haunts me like it never left,
was i just a lesson to them?
them, so many people
too many eyes looking into my soul
was i just a lesson to you all?

you played the game and won
got to know what not to do
don't have friends
don't fall in love with a poet
don't have a daughter
don't be kind
don't be
human
don't
don't
don't.

but you did that already
so who really lost? what was lost?
love lost
thrown away into the pit but you forget, it's my home
even when the light of hatred touches love,
and they glow fire in the darkness,
even if they burn me,
i'll cradle them laying down on this earth.

—

chapter six: the healing

39. a eulogy to my hands

you had felt more than enough so i had to,

i had to let you go; to free you from my cages,

they told me to prepare a eulogy for you; i didn't know how to, for you have always worked on your own whim and bled words on the paper,

now in the middle of the night, the only marks on it are my tears,

i am made to remember all those mornings when i made you claw at my face with uncut fingernails; all those afternoons when i forced you to grope the skin on my tummy in disappointment; all those nights when i couldn't stop whimpering in heartache where you were the only one wiping away my tears; your touch was gentle, loving, even though i had you cut open my thighs multiple times; when i bruised your knuckles angrily punching the walls,

i only ever put knives, blades, hate in your palm but all you ever did was try to make me love me;

it was love i know in all your actions; when you weren't disgusted by my unwashed hair and softly ran your fingers through it under the warm shower; when you guided me to eat because it doesn't matter if i gain weight: when you made me put your palm on my tummy and give it little pats; when you painted my face with different colors helping me express

myself better; all you've ever known to do is love me and i
made you a tool in my hatred,
but now as i dictate the tale to my friend for them to write,
i make a promise;
i will fulfill your wish; *i will love myself.*

40. the call of elpis

sometimes, i feel like drowning,

others, i feel like saving myself, just riding the waves,

desperately holding on to the weeds,

my feet digging in the sand,

my mind forcing me to not jump in the water,

but suddenly im going under,

the earth beneath opens up and swallows me whole,

i hear someone call my name, it's elpis,

she takes my hand in hers,

we walk through the water

there, appears a cottage,

covered with hyacinths, daisies, violets, crocuses and irises,

she tells me to look inside,

through the boarded window,

i was looking at someone's back, they turn around as if someone called out their name,

i gasp in surprise, it was me, but a bit older,

she's cooking for the three people seated at the table, i can't see their faces,

then he looks right into my eyes, i panic and hide,

they call out my name,

now i can see everyone,

it's them,

the lover is standing beside her, aimlessly kissing their head,

the wife and the sister sitting,

all of them smiling but still looking at me with yearning eyes,

elpis puts her hand on my eyes,

images drift by,

are these flashbacks? no, it's the future,

laughing at the kitchen table, card games in the lounge,

teaching at the local library,

poetry readings,

them,

elpis softly reminds me "blood of the covenant is thicker than the water of the womb"

she now holds me, i open my eyes and everything is gone,

im no longer under water,

i cry out for them,

elpis silences me "they're still going to be there, child. it's upto you now,

do you want to drown in the turbulent waves of the water of the womb?"

no i don't,

i will hold on, even if the weeds give up and snap, i will hold on,

i will hold on to see that sunrise with them,

to see the moonrise too,

we're bound by blood, melancholy, anger and love,

now, with our tears, sedum and protea will bloom everlastingly

—

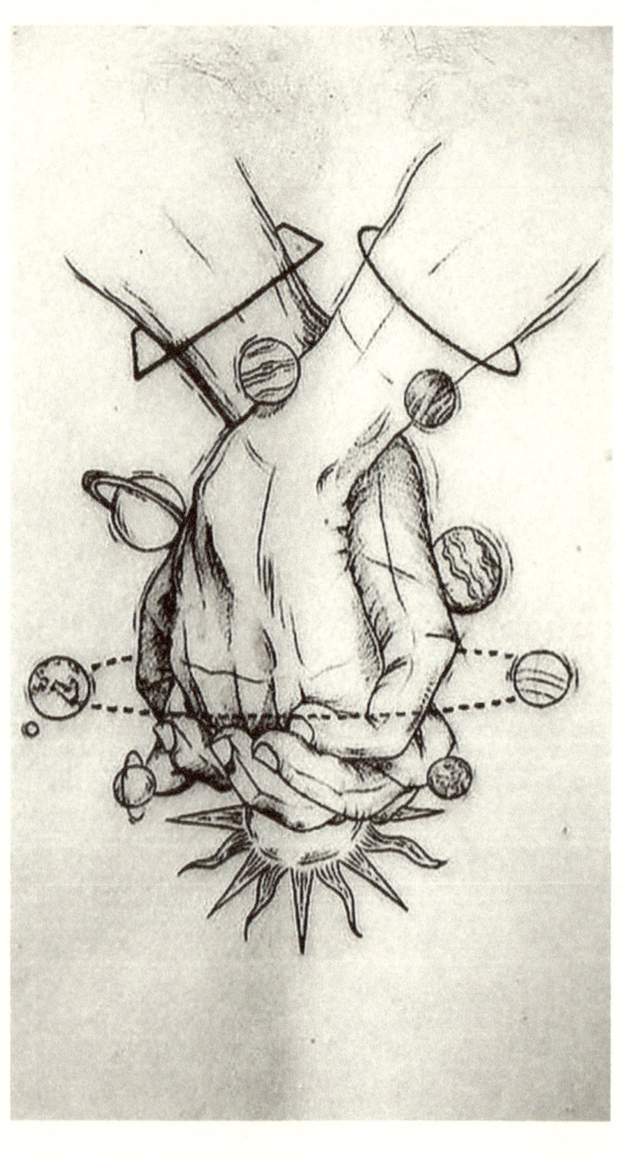

41. i live in you//you live in me

i stand before you
with a hollow chest,
my hands bloody for i ripped my heart
out for you,
it worked without a purpose all this time,
the beat had no melody,
i saw you and i felt for the first time what being alive was,
you merely touched me and my heart ached to jump in your
arms as if it already knew you,
my entire self was yours before it was mine,
you gently hold the bleeding heart close to yours,
you decide my fate,
i will die with you,
i will live for you,
you look into my eyes,
a look that feels like a strong embrace,
i hear your voice in myself,
"we'll live in love" you say,
you hear my voice in you,
"we'll live in love."

42. when you and me met

you and me met after knowing each other for mere months,
so why did it feel like we've known each other all along?
maybe it's because we found the other during a vulnerable time,
i don't think we'll ever get an answer,

you and me met, you were a bit late because you came from far away,
why did my nervous heart calmed down when i saw you see me?
maybe it's because you've become a safe space,
i don't think we'll ever get an answer,

you and me met, you hugged me first,
why did you still do it even after i told you the scorching heat made me sweat?
maybe it's because you wanted to make sure that i was real,
i don't think we'll ever get an answer,

you and me met, i gave you the fake purple orchids,
because i couldn't find the real ones,
why did you steal my line by saying that this way you can keep them with you longer?

maybe it's because our minds have connected,
i don't think we'll ever get an answer,

you and me met, and you left with a hug,
why did your eyes look the way they did when you told me to
take care and get back home safe?
maybe it was pure love in them,
i don't think we'll ever get an answer,

you and me met, i was sitting in the uber,
why did i feel like crying at that time?
i don't think we'll ever get an answer,

you and me met, i was sitting in the uber
why couldn't i tell the driver to stop trying to make
conversation with me, for if i opened my mouth any longer, i
would burst into tears?
i don't think we'll ever get an answer,

you and me met, after coming back to my house,
i realized that i love you wholeheartedly and us parting ways
even for the time being felt like my soul was being cut up,
i got my answer that somewhere along the fateful path, you
became my home.

43. the tea will be warm whenever you want to visit

the thunder almost overpowers the sound of the bell
not knowing who to expect at this hour,
i open the door,
the confusion in my eyes turns into a smile
immediately after seeing your face
i didn't know where to go
i'm sorry if i disturbed you
shush, come in
you're always welcome,
you know that
sit down,
no need to worry about wetting the couch
it'll dry,
let me get you a hand towel for your hair
it's longer now
yours is still short [as how i liked it]
here you go, freshen up
you were eating,
i must have interrupted your night
i should get going
no please stay for a little while
wait till the storm lets up

i have one more seat at the table for you

i'll make you a sandwich,

of course with no ketchup

you remember

i remember

i would offer you a cup of coffee

but you don't drink it,

would green tea work?

always so ready to take care of people

yes, i would love some tea

coming right up!

we giggle at the same time

your crinkling eyes have always been so beautiful

eat up

you were hungry, weren't you?

the rain stopped

i see, are you leaving then?

yes, thank you for-

i know, don't mention it

and listen?

yes, love?

i'll be here with sandwiches whenever

there's a storm and you're around.

44. an aubade for me

i no longer wish to dip my pen in blood,
the paper doesn't have to be torn,
i will use the flowers, the colors,
the stem of a daisy to write,
it'll be delicate,
it'll be beautiful,
it won't howl in pain,
the words won't yell at you to look at them,
it'll be so ethereal that your eyes won't stray away,
they'll whisper in your ears, like the ocean breeze,
like how your lover lulls you to sleep,
like the way you softly touch a baby's hands,
like the gentle way, a mother braids her kids' hair,
a soft kiss on the forehead at the end of the evening,
not a goodbye,
a promise to meet again

—

About The Author

aph;muski has been properly writing ever since she was sixteen years old but their love for reading had begun way back. the name "aph;muski" started off as a way to sign poetry but now the name has become her identity signifying the growth from a kid to an adult but still being connected to their roots. a true literature nerd and with godlike abilities, aph keeps on creating masterpieces. you can connect with her on instagram, the handle is @knj.rmeo.

Message To Readers

if reading my words made you feel, be it sadness, happiness, yearning for something you never had but so very much deserve, anger for the ones who hurt you, anger for me, if my words made you feel vulnerable to an uncomfortable extent, made you feel heard, not alone, in love again, anything at all then, my existence as a poet is proven to be worthy.

thank you for taking a glimpse into my soul.

Space To Annotate Your Heart Out (1)

Space To Annotate Your Heart Out (2)

Space To Annotate Your Heart Out (3)

Space To Annotate Your Heart Out (4)